SECURE YOUR CIRCLE

GODLY BOUNDARIES THAT LEAD TO PROSPERITY

SECURE YOUR CIRCLE:

GODLY BOUNDARIES THAT LEAD TO PROSPERITY

TOM CORNELL

 First edition.

Paperback ISBN: 978-1-969882-35-7

CONTENTS

INTRODUCTION

THE BLESSING IS IN THE BOUNDARY

We live in a culture that celebrates being constantly available, perpetually giving, and endlessly involved. But here's the truth no one wants to admit: you can't carry what God didn't assign to you. Many believers are burned out, broke, or burdened—not because they're disobedient, but because they're overextended. They're living outside of grace because they're living outside of their God-given boundaries.

Somewhere along the way, we confused compassion with chaos and equated spirituality with sacrifice that violates our covenants. We thought we were being like Jesus, but we were acting like saviors. And when you try to be someone's savior, you're walking in disobedience to the One who actually is.

This book is a confrontation to that mindset. It's an invitation to realign with God's divine order so that your life, family, finances, and ministry can move from survival to supernatural provision. The Kingdom of God is not a chaotic free-for-all. It's a government—a divine order—with boundaries, stewardship, and responsibility. And wherever there is divine order, there is divine blessing.

Jesus made a bold promise in Matthew 6:33:

"Seek first the Kingdom of God and His righteousness, and all these things will be added to you."

The key to prosperity isn't found in hustling harder. It's found in seeking His Kingdom first and staying under His authority. That means knowing what is yours to carry—and what isn't.

Many people are praying for more when God is asking them to steward better. They want promotion without alignment. Increase without order. Influence without responsibility. But in the Kingdom, that's not how it works. God increases what we protect, not what we neglect. And He breathes on what is properly aligned, not what is emotionally reactive.

The problem is that most people don't know where their God-given circle of responsibility begins—or ends. They're entangled in the needs of others, constantly drained by guilt-driven giving, and overwhelmed by obligations they were never meant to carry. They've never been taught that boundaries are biblical. That stewardship is spiritual. That you cannot save the world if you can't pay your own bills.

But what if God has already assigned you a "circle"?
A realm of responsibility?
A specific area of authority?

And what if your breakthrough, your blessing, and your

overflow are waiting on you to secure that circle—and stop living outside it? This book will help you:

- Define your circle of responsibility
- Break free from the trap of emotional, unbiblical giving
- Discern between covenant and compassion
- Build healthy boundaries in relationships, finances, and ministry
- Prosper by focusing on what God has entrusted to you
- Stop spiritualizing chaos and start living in order and overflow

You'll also discover how the enemy works overtime to blur boundaries—because he knows if you ever get clear, you'll get powerful. When your life is built around obedience, not obligation—faith, not fear—you'll finally stop leaking energy, money, and peace into places God never called you to sustain.

So here's the foundational principle of this entire book:
Prosperity doesn't begin with more—it begins with clarity.

You don't need to do more.
You don't need to give more.
You need to know what's yours and steward it well.

You were never called to rescue everyone, fix everything, or carry what isn't yours. You were called to walk in authority where God has assigned you. And when you do that—when you secure your circle—you will prosper.

Let's begin.

CHAPTER 1

SEEK FIRST THE KINGDOM —AND STAY IN RANK

There is a divine order to everything God does. From creation to covenant, from the tabernacle to the church, God's pattern is always built on order, alignment, and intentionality. And when we align with that divine order, heaven begins to flow in our lives in ways we could never manufacture by striving.

Jesus made it clear:

"Seek first the Kingdom of God and His righteousness, and all these things shall be added to you" (Matthew 6:33).

This isn't a motivational verse—it's a blueprint for life. Jesus wasn't offering a religious suggestion. He was revealing a spiritual law: everything added to your life is connected to what you seek first.

You can seek money and never find peace.
You can chase relationships and still feel empty.

But when you seek the Kingdom—His rule, His order, His government—everything you truly need is added.

Kingdom First Means Rank First

Seeking first doesn't mean seeking only. It means putting everything else under the rule of the One who reigns. It's not about quitting your job to read Scripture all day. It's about placing your entire life under divine alignment: your thoughts, relationships, time, finances, home, ministry, business—everything.

The word "Kingdom" implies government. It's not chaotic or random. It's structured and ranked. It's not just spiritual goosebumps or emotional highs—it's a system where authority flows through honor, obedience, and proper alignment. And when your life comes under that system, provision flows where submission goes.

That's why Jesus didn't say, "Try harder and I'll add things to you." He said, "Seek My Kingdom first." Prioritize it. Honor it. Submit to it. Come into rank with it. And watch what heaven adds.

Alignment Before Assignment

Before God gives assignment, He checks alignment.

When God created Adam, He didn't give him a global ministry. He gave him a garden. He didn't say, "Fill the heavens." He said, "Be fruitful and multiply... and have dominion over the earth" (Genesis 1:28). Why? Because God blesses what He delegates, not what we assume.

Adam was given boundaries—a circle to steward. Eden was not the whole earth. It was a space within the earth. Prosperity would begin there, and through faithful stewardship, expand. God always starts with the specific before He blesses the broad.

You'll never walk in true authority until you walk in alignment with God's delegated order. And you'll never experience consistent provision outside of your assigned circle.

Many people pray for increase but resist order. They want multiplication without submission. They crave overflow without rank. But in the Kingdom, blessing follows obedience, not busyness. Clarity precedes capacity. And honor precedes harvest.

Why Some Things Haven't Been "Added"

If you've ever wondered why you're not seeing breakthrough in a certain area, this question must be asked: Is this area under the rule of God's Kingdom? Or is it governed by emotion, fear, pride, or survival?

Because the promise of Matthew 6:33 isn't a blanket guarantee for every Christian—it's a covenant principle for those who walk in order. "All these things will be added to you" is only true if you are walking in the pursuit of Kingdom-first living.

Here's the sobering truth:
God doesn't add to disorder.
He doesn't increase what's out of alignment.

He doesn't bless what we're pretending to steward while actually avoiding responsibility. If you're sowing, serving, and sacrificing—but not seeing return—don't first assume the devil is blocking your harvest. Ask instead:

- Am I under proper authority?
- Have I surrendered this area to God's rule?
- Have I placed it first under His priorities, not just my preferences?

The Kingdom is not just about power—it's about protocol.

Living Under Authority Releases Authority

Authority isn't about control. It's about covering. And God's blessing flows through the covering of His Kingdom. Just as water flows through pipes that are properly aligned, the provision of God flows through systems and lives that are in divine order.

Jesus modeled this perfectly. Though fully God, He walked in submission to the Father. He said, "I only do what I see the Father doing" and "My food is to do the will of Him who sent Me." He understood that true authority flows from relational submission.

You can't claim Kingdom results while rejecting Kingdom order.

If Jesus walked under authority to release power, how much more must we?

When your life is under the authority of God's rule, your circle of influence becomes a place where heaven touches earth. Your home carries peace. Your finances multiply. Your family flourishes. Your decisions flow with clarity. Not because you did more—but because you aligned more.

Provision Is Attached to Your Position

We've been taught that provision follows passion. But the Kingdom teaches that provision follows position. Where you are aligned determines what you receive.

This is why some believers serve endlessly in areas they were never assigned to—and still experience lack. Others give sacrificially out of guilt and see no return. They are operating out of emotion, not out of authority.

When you get into your assigned place—your Eden—everything you need to steward it well will be added to you. But the moment you step outside your circle and try to control what isn't yours, the grace lifts. You'll feel the drain. You'll carry burdens that were never meant for you. You'll confuse chaos with compassion.

But when you stay in your God-given lane—seeking first His Kingdom and staying in proper rank—provision flows like water. It may not always be easy, but it will always be covered.

Key Questions to Discern Kingdom Alignment:

- Have I submitted this area of my life to God's rule?
- Am I trying to provide for myself outside of His timing and boundaries?
- Is this responsibility mine—or something I've taken on from pressure or guilt?
- Am I walking in the right place, at the right time, under the right authority?

If the answer to these questions reveals disorder, don't panic. God is not the author of confusion—but He is the God of clarity. And when you repent, realign, and reprioritize, the blessings begin to flow again.

Application: Stay in Rank, Stay in Flow

You don't need more to prosper—you need order.
You don't need to hustle—you need to honor.
You don't need to be everywhere—you need to be where God assigned you.

Prosperity isn't found in more effort. It's found in staying under authority and stewarding what's yours.

The moment you put God's Kingdom first and submit your whole life to His government, something shifts. You go from surviving to stewarding. From striving to receiving. From chaos to clarity.

God is not trying to hide prosperity from you—He's trying to build it through you. But it starts with one choice:

Seek first the Kingdom.
And stay in rank.

CHAPTER 2

YOU HAVE A CIRCLE—AND IT'S YOURS TO GUARD

Before you can steward something well, you must first know what belongs to you. One of the greatest sources of burnout in the lives of sincere believers is not rebellion—it's confusion about responsibility. They're carrying things God never called them to carry. They're fighting battles they were never assigned. They're exhausted from pouring into people, projects, and places that lie outside of their God-given circle.

God is not chaotic. He's not ambiguous. He assigns responsibility on purpose. And where there is divine assignment, there is divine authority.

The key to walking in peace, provision, and power is found in one question: What is in your circle?

The First Commission: Dominion, Not Co-Dependency

In Genesis 1:28, we read the original mandate given to humanity:

"Be fruitful and multiply, fill the earth and subdue it; have dominion..."

From the beginning, God gave humans the authority to rule —but not over everything, and not without limit. Adam and Eve were placed in a specific garden in a specific region and were given charge over it. They were not called to rule the world on Day One. They were assigned a defined space to steward and protect.

That is still God's pattern today.

Every believer is given a circle of dominion—a specific realm where they are called to exercise authority, walk in stewardship, and cultivate fruitfulness. That circle might include:

- Your home
- Your spouse
- Your children
- Your finances
- Your business
- Your health
- Your time
- Your emotional life
- Your covenant relationships

If God gave it to you, He also gave you the grace to manage it. And the health of your life depends on recognizing what's yours to manage—and what's not.

The Trap of Over-Responsibility

The enemy doesn't always use temptation to take believers out. Sometimes, he uses compassion out of bounds. If he can't get you to sin, he'll try to get you to over-function—to pour your time, energy, and resources into things that drain you instead of things you were called to develop.

We often confuse love with obligation. We think being helpful means saying "yes" to everyone and everything. But here's the reality: You cannot effectively care for what's inside your circle if you're constantly giving attention to what's outside of it.

God did not assign you to fix everyone's marriage.
God did not call you to save every addict.
God did not ask you to carry the emotional weight of people who refuse to change.

He asked you to steward your circle.

Compassion doesn't mean codependency.
Love doesn't mean burnout.
Ministry doesn't mean martyrdom.

Jesus loved the world—but He still withdrew. He still slept in storms. He still said "no" to people who wanted His time when it wasn't His assignment. Why? Because He only did what the Father told Him to do. That's true Kingdom alignment.

Clarity Creates Freedom

The moment you identify what is inside your circle, you are freed from the pressure of what's outside it. You're released from the burden of trying to rescue people who belong to God, not to you. And you're empowered to give your best to the things you've actually been entrusted with.

Ask yourself:

- What has God assigned to me in this season?
- What responsibilities are mine, and which ones are emotional leftovers from past seasons or misplaced expectations?
- Where am I overreaching?

God is not looking for frantic people who say "yes" to everything. He's looking for faithful stewards who know their assignment and guard it well.

The Circle Exercise: Drawing the Line

Take a moment to literally draw a circle on a piece of paper.

Inside the circle, write everything you know God has entrusted to you right now. Be specific. Include:

- People (by covenant or care: spouse, children, employees, spiritual sons/daughters)
- Properties or possessions (home, car, bank account)
- Ministries or roles (pastor, leader, business owner, etc.)
- Personal well-being (your body, mind, and spirit)

Outside the circle, write things you may care about—but aren't directly responsible for. These could include:

- Adults making repeated destructive choices
- Social media opinions and online drama
- Other people's expectations of your time
- Issues in churches or ministries you don't lead
- Financial crises you didn't cause

Once that circle is drawn, pause and reflect:

- Where have I been investing time and energy outside my circle?
- What's suffering inside my circle because I'm distracted by what's outside it?
- What boundaries do I need to enforce?

Then pray over your circle. Ask the Holy Spirit to help you become a fierce steward of what's yours—and to release the false responsibility for what's not.

Boundaries Guard What You're Building

If you were building a house, you wouldn't leave it open to every passerby. You would install locks, place fences, and set alarms—not because you're unloving, but because what you're building matters.

Your circle is your house. Your boundaries are your walls.

And here's the truth: you can't build without boundaries. You can't prosper while leaving every window open to whoever knocks. You can't steward your finances, family, or faith if your energy is constantly leaking into unassigned territory.

The enemy doesn't need to destroy your calling. He just needs to distract you from it. And distraction almost always looks like a "good thing"—a person in need, a last-minute crisis, a favor, a request, a demand that you feel too guilty to say no to.

But if you say "yes" to everyone else, you will eventually say "no" to what God asked you to build.

What Happens When You Guard Your Circle

When you clarify your circle and commit to protecting it, powerful things begin to happen:

- Peace increases. You're no longer spread thin by everyone else's chaos.
- Provision flows. God releases resources to what He's assigned.
- Health is restored. You can pour into your own soul again.
- Authority grows. When you steward the small well, God entrusts more.
- Freedom returns. You realize you're not responsible to fix what isn't yours.

This is not selfishness—it's stewardship. This is not isolation—it's intentional alignment with heaven.

Boundaries are not about exclusion. They're about faithfully guarding what's been entrusted to you so that you can multiply it.

Your Circle Is Sacred

You may not think your home, your marriage, your business, or your bank account are spiritual battlegrounds—but they are. What's in your circle is sacred. And what's sacred must be guarded with wisdom, not guilt.

When Nehemiah rebuilt the wall around Jerusalem, he didn't start by praying for revival. He started by defining boundaries. He repaired the gates. He stationed people in front of their homes. He told the builders to hold a weapon in one hand and a tool in the other.

Why? Because if you don't protect what you're building, the enemy will destroy it while you're trying to finish it.

You don't just need vision. You need vigilance.

God Blesses What You Guard

Let this truth sink in: God blesses what you guard.

He blesses marriages that are protected from emotional adultery.

He blesses homes where leadership is clear and boundaries are enforced.

He blesses finances that are stewarded with diligence, not distributed through guilt.

He blesses ministries where leaders stay in their lane and protect their priorities.

He blesses parents who don't give their kids everything, but teach them stewardship.

He blesses believers who know their circle and stand watch over it.

If the enemy has been robbing you of time, peace, energy, or money, it's time to redraw the line.

Get clear. Get honest. Get aligned.

You don't need to do more. You need to guard what's yours.

CHAPTER 3

PERSONAL RESPONSIBILITY UNLOCKS SPIRITUAL AUTHORITY

Authority in the Kingdom of God doesn't come from titles, charisma, or even knowledge. It flows from responsibility. Heaven recognizes and responds to those who faithfully steward what they've been entrusted with. When you take ownership of your circle—your family, finances, home, calling—you gain spiritual authority in that realm. But when you avoid responsibility or abandon stewardship, you forfeit authority.

The problem isn't always that believers are disobedient. It's often that they are irresponsible—waiting for breakthrough while neglecting the order that makes breakthrough possible.

In the Kingdom, you cannot walk in power without walking in responsibility.

Authority Follows Assignment

Jesus said in Luke 16:10, *"Whoever can be trusted with little can also be trusted with much."* This wasn't just a lesson on money—

it was a spiritual law. God promotes those who protect. He increases what is rightly handled. And He expands influence where faithfulness has been proven.

You don't need more power—you need more ownership.

The enemy's goal is not just to tempt you into sin; it's to keep you distracted and passive so that you never step into the authority you've been given. He wants you to avoid responsibility, blame others, and live in a cycle of victimhood. Why? Because as long as you stay passive, you stay powerless.

But the moment you take full responsibility for what's in your circle, you become dangerous to darkness.

The Lie of Power Without Stewardship

Many believers want to cast out demons but can't manage their calendar.

They want to lead people to Jesus but can't lead their own emotions.

They want God to bless their business but won't take inventory of their spending.

Here's the hard truth: God will not bless what you refuse to take responsibility for.

If you're asking for favor in areas you've not been stewarding, heaven is silent—not because God is angry, but because God is just. The Kingdom doesn't operate on hype. It operates on principle and alignment.

There is no shortcut to authority. And there is no substitute for stewardship.

Responsibility: The Gateway to Dominion

Let's go back to Genesis 1:28. The commission was to "be fruitful, multiply, fill the earth, subdue it, and have dominion." This was a process, not an instant reality. Fruitfulness comes first. Dominion comes later.

In other words, before you take dominion, you must first prove yourself fruitful.

Fruitfulness only comes through responsibility. You must tend the garden before you rule the territory. You must steward the seed before you manage the harvest. You must govern your circle before you're trusted with broader influence.

Fruitfulness is proof of stewardship. And stewardship is what unlocks dominion.

Spiritual Authority Is Territorial

Every person is given a realm of authority—a circle—by God. That realm is not just physical, but spiritual. When you take responsibility for it, you gain spiritual authority within it.

For example:

- A parent who faithfully disciples their children gains authority in their family.
- A business owner who honors God and leads with integrity gains authority in the marketplace.
- A pastor who doesn't just preach but cares for people gains authority in the spirit over that region.

- A believer who manages their money wisely gains authority to fund Kingdom initiatives.

But the moment you abdicate responsibility, your authority leaks.

You cannot cast out spirits in someone else's house if your own house is in chaos.

You cannot declare breakthrough over finances you refuse to budget.

You cannot expect peace in your home while tolerating emotional disorder.

Authority follows alignment. And alignment starts with ownership.

The Enemy Exploits Irresponsibility

Satan is a legalist. He seeks to exploit any gap where responsibility has been abandoned. He loves to enter through doors that believers refuse to close.

If you don't take responsibility for your emotional health, he will sow division in your relationships.

If you don't take responsibility for your finances, he will torment you with lack and fear.

If you don't take responsibility for your time, he will fill your schedule with distractions.

If you don't take responsibility for your spiritual life, he will lead you into apathy and dullness.

Responsibility is your spiritual armor. It closes the gaps. It seals the cracks. It tells the enemy, "I am aware of what's mine, and I will steward it with diligence and prayer."

Stewardship Is Not Control—It's Alignment

Some believers avoid responsibility because they confuse it with control. But control is rooted in fear. Stewardship is rooted in faith.

Stewardship doesn't mean you force outcomes—it means you faithfully manage what's in your hand. You cannot make your children obey, but you can disciple them and create a home of peace. You cannot force people to stay in relationship with you, but you can walk in honor, humility, and forgiveness.

You are not God. But you are God's steward.

And when you show God that you will protect what He has entrusted to you, He will entrust you with more.

Faithfulness Is the Fast Track to Favor

Many are praying for doors to open—but God is waiting for them to lock the ones they left open.

Favor doesn't fall randomly. It follows those who walk in faithfulness. And faithfulness is not about being perfect—it's about being present, intentional, and aligned with Heaven.

Ask yourself:

- Am I managing my time with purpose?

- Am I nurturing my relationships with consistency?
- Am I sowing into my family, finances, and faith life?
- Am I present to the responsibilities I've been given?

When you say "yes" to what's yours, heaven says "yes" to your authority.

Stewardship Is the Soil Where Authority Grows

Just like a seed needs soil, water, and light to grow, authority grows in the soil of stewardship.

You don't need to promote yourself.

You don't need to shout louder.

You need to be faithful with what's in your hand.

Remember the parable of the talents. The master didn't reward the servant who had the most. He rewarded the one who multiplied what he was given. The wicked servant wasn't condemned for stealing—he was condemned for doing nothing.

"You wicked and lazy servant..."

Laziness is not neutral—it's wickedness in disguise. It's the refusal to engage with your God-given responsibilities.

You Are Not the Savior—But You Are the Steward

Taking responsibility doesn't mean rescuing everyone. It means responding to God with faithfulness in what He's entrusted to you.

You don't have to fix everyone's life.

You don't have to carry everyone's burden.

You just have to manage what's yours and do it well.

Your job is not to be Jesus. Your job is to partner with Jesus in stewarding what He's placed in your circle.

Practical Activation: Inventory Your Responsibilities

Make a list this week:

1. What has God placed in my hands to steward?
2. Where have I been neglecting responsibility—through avoidance, procrastination, or passivity?
3. Where have I been trying to walk in authority without first walking in alignment?
4. What boundaries do I need to reinforce to protect my responsibilities?
5. Who or what have I been trying to "fix" that is not mine to manage?

Then pray:

"Father, help me to take full responsibility for what You've entrusted to me.

Let me not delay, deny, or deflect what's mine to steward.

And as I align with Your order, release authority and grace to prosper in every area of my circle. In Jesus' name, amen."

You're Not Waiting on God—God Is Waiting on You

You don't need more anointing to walk in authority.
You don't need more money to live in prosperity.
You need to own your assignment and steward your circle.
The mantle of authority is waiting.
Heaven is ready to partner with you.
But it will not anoint passivity.
It will anoint responsibility.

So rise up. Take ownership. Guard your circle. And watch how authority begins to flow like never before.

CHAPTER 4

COVENANTS COME FIRST

LOVE BEGINS AT HOME

You cannot walk in Kingdom prosperity while neglecting Kingdom order. And Kingdom order always prioritizes covenant over compassion, commitment over emotion, and foundation before expansion. Many believers struggle financially and relationally not because they don't love God, but because they are pouring out to the world while letting their own house fall apart.

Love is not supposed to start on the mission field, in the church building, or on the group chat. It starts at home.

If your life is out of order, your generosity will be out of order. If your priorities are misaligned, your provision will be too. This chapter is a call back to the foundation of prosperity: keeping covenant.

The Snare of Rash Vows

Proverbs 20:25 warns,

"It is a snare to dedicate something rashly and only later to consider one's vows."

In other words, it's a trap to commit without counting the cost. And yet, how often do we give our "yes" emotionally, only to realize later we can't afford what we've vowed—financially, relationally, or spiritually?

Emotion says, "I have to help."
Wisdom says, "Let me see if I have the capacity to help."
The Kingdom says, "Fulfill your covenants first—then give with clarity."

God doesn't bless emotion. He blesses obedience.

Covenant First, Then Overflow

Prosperity isn't found in spontaneous sacrifice. It's found in ordered giving. That means you give after your covenantal obligations are fulfilled—not instead of them.

Here's the hard but liberating truth: To give when you haven't fulfilled your covenants is not generosity—it's theft.

Yes, that sounds intense. But it's Biblical.

- If you're giving to a friend while behind on your rent, you're robbing your landlord.
- If you're helping cover someone else's bills while your spouse is begging you to get out of debt, you're breaking covenant.
- If you're funding a ministry trip while owing your child support, you are out of alignment with heaven.

The world might applaud your "sacrifice," but heaven sees disobedience. God will not fund disorder.

False Guilt Leads to Foolish Giving

Some of the most dangerous giving is done not out of love, but out of guilt.

Guilt giving looks like:

- Saying yes to financial requests you feel uneasy about
- Feeling pressure to give because you don't want to seem "selfish"
- Trying to rescue someone from consequences God is using to mature them
- Giving money to cover dysfunction instead of sowing into transformation

Giving out of guilt is not righteousness. It's often codependency wearing a religious mask.

True giving should be Spirit-led, covenant-protected, and wisdom-filtered.

You were never meant to solve everyone's problems—especially not at the expense of your own household.

Misplaced Generosity Steals from Covenant

Let's take it even further. Giving to others before fulfilling your covenant responsibilities is not only unwise—it's unjust.

The Bible teaches that we are to owe no one anything

(Romans 13:8), and that a righteous person keeps their word even when it hurts (Psalm 15:4).

That means paying your bills is holy.

That means following through on a business agreement is worship.

That means showing up for your spouse and your children is a prophetic act.

We don't always associate things like paying rent or covering payroll as spiritual—but in the Kingdom, every covenant matters.

God is not moved by your emotional desire to help someone else if you're neglecting someone you already vowed to care for.

"Love Your Neighbor" Doesn't Cancel Responsibility

Jesus said to love your neighbor—but not at the cost of the ones you're already bound to by covenant.

You're not called to love your neighbor more than your spouse.

You're not called to rescue the poor while your kids are starving for your attention.

You're not called to be available to everyone while being absent from your assignment.

The enemy loves to twist "love" into obligation and "generosity" into irresponsibility. But true love honors order. It respects priority. And it starts with faithfulness to the people and promises in your life.

Financial Covenant Check

Here's a practical filter: Before you give, ask yourself:

- Have I paid my bills this month?
- Have I met my financial obligations to my spouse, children, or employees?
- Am I giving out of margin or robbing from my responsibilities?
- Is this gift motivated by love—or guilt, pressure, or fear?

If the answer reveals misalignment, don't give yet. God will never ask you to be generous in a way that violates your responsibilities.

He's not trying to break your bank—He's trying to build your foundation.

What About Helping the Needy?

Of course, we are called to care for the poor, support ministry, and sow into Kingdom initiatives. But giving to the needy should come from overflow, not obligation. The parable of the Good Samaritan wasn't about someone going into debt to save a stranger. It was about someone who had margin—emotional, financial, and time margin—to stop and help.

That's the kind of giver God wants you to become: not reactive, but ready.

You can't give freely if your own circle is on fire. You can't respond to divine appointments if your life is filled with man-made emergencies. You can't carry others if your foundation is cracking.

Prosperity begins with getting your house in order.

Build the Altar at Home First

When Elijah repaired the altar in 1 Kings 18, he didn't call down fire first. He restored what had been broken. He set the stones in place. Then he dug the trenches. Then he poured the water. Then he placed the sacrifice.

Only after the altar was in order did fire fall from heaven.

You want fire in your life?
Start by putting your altar in order.

That means honoring your marriage.
Paying what you owe.
Fulfilling your word.
Protecting your covenant relationships.
Building your house—before blessing someone else's.

Covenant = Priority

Here's the pattern:

1. God first – Your obedience, tithe, worship, surrender.
2. Your household – Marriage, family, home, children.
3. Your inner circle – Close friendships, spiritual family.
4. Your Kingdom assignment – Ministry, marketplace, service.

5. Others in need – As the Spirit leads and as capacity allows.

This is not selfishness—it's righteous prioritization. When you give from a strong foundation, your giving is sustainable and powerful.

Stop Leaking Blessing—Secure Your Vows

If your finances feel like a bucket with holes, check your covenants.

Are you keeping your word?
Are you paying your bills on time?
Are you faithful in the small things?
Are you being generous to strangers while neglecting your spouse?

Plug the leaks before asking for more water.

Heaven honors those who honor their vows.

Prosperity Comes Through Covenant-Keeping

You can't build a lasting life on broken promises.

The fastest way to invite poverty is to break covenant. The fastest way to attract blessing is to keep it—faithfully, quietly, daily.

You don't need to go viral. You don't need to impress crowds. You need to show up where you're planted and fulfill what you've promised.

In a world of flashy giving and performative generosity, God is looking for covenant-keepers—those who will protect their home, guard their word, and live in alignment with their responsibilities.

And when you do that, you will prosper—not just financially, but spiritually, emotionally, and relationally.

Activation: Covenant Inventory

Take inventory this week. Make three lists:

1. Covenants I've made – Marriage, family, business, ministry.
2. Obligations I owe – Bills, debts, payroll, tithe, commitments.
3. Ways I've broken or neglected those covenants – Missed payments, avoidance, neglect.

Then ask:

- Am I pretending to be generous while avoiding what I owe?
- Am I seeking applause or approval while neglecting those closest to me?
- What is one covenant I need to restore or honor this week?

Pray:

"Father, forgive me for putting emotion over order, guilt over obedience, and people over priority. Help me to honor every covenant You've entrusted to me. Teach me to give from alignment, not pressure. Let my love start at home. And let my generosity flow from a place of strength, not striving. In Jesus' name, amen."

CHAPTER 5

DISCERNMENT IN GIVING

COMPASSION ISN'T CHAOS

Generosity is powerful, but when it's detached from discernment, it becomes dangerous. Many believers are depleted—not because they're disobedient, but because they've been unwise in their giving. They confuse compassion with calling, and emotion with assignment. But in the Kingdom, giving isn't just about how much—it's about where, why, and when.

Compassion is holy. Chaos is not.
Giving is godly. Guilt is not.
Sacrifice is beautiful. Striving is not.

This chapter is about learning to give with discernment. To stop giving reactively and start giving righteously. Because in the Kingdom, not every need is your responsibility—and not every ask is your assignment.

The Difference Between Spirit-Led Giving and Soul-Led Giving

Let's define the two:

- Spirit-led giving is intentional, prayerful, and aligned with your assignment. It produces fruit, peace, and long-term blessing.
- Soul-led giving is reactive, emotional, and guilt-driven. It produces anxiety, confusion, and often resentment.

Soul-led giving usually feels urgent and overwhelming. You feel cornered, shamed, or manipulated into giving. It sounds like:

- "If you really loved me..."
- "You're the only one who can help."
- "God told me you were supposed to give."

None of those are how the Holy Spirit operates. God doesn't guilt. He guides.

You are not called to respond to every need. You're called to respond to the Spirit.

"To Give When You Owe Is to Steal"

Here's a hard truth that many believers have never heard:

To give to someone else when you have unmet responsibilities is not generosity—it's theft.

You're robbing from your landlord, your spouse, your business, or your family to meet a need God never assigned to you. That kind of giving creates disorder, not blessing.

Scripture says:
"If anyone does not provide for his own, especially for his household, he has denied the faith and is worse than an unbeliever."
(1 Timothy 5:8)

That's a strong rebuke—not against unbelievers, but against believers who are giving in the name of ministry while neglecting their basic responsibilities.

When you understand this, it changes how you give:

- You stop sacrificing your family's peace to help someone who refuses to take ownership.
- You stop giving money you need for bills just to avoid confrontation.
- You stop responding to emotional pleas that were never your burden to carry.

Real generosity begins with alignment, not emotion.

When Compassion Becomes Compromise

It's possible to give in a way that actually enables dysfunction. You think you're helping, but you're actually propping up poor decisions, avoiding confrontation, or delaying someone's growth.

Here are a few signs your giving has become compromise:

- You're constantly giving to the same person, but their life never changes.
- You feel resentment after you give.
- You're hiding your giving from your spouse or team.

- You're overextended financially but feel guilty saying "no."

God never called you to be everyone's breakthrough. He called you to be obedient.

That means sometimes your "no" is just as Spirit-led as your "yes."

That means sometimes the most loving thing you can do is withhold, pray, and trust that God is working.

The Trap of Emotional Giving

Emotional giving sounds spiritual, but it's often flesh dressed up as faith. It bypasses wisdom and stewardship. It's often based on appearance and urgency, not truth.

This is how people get manipulated into:

- Supporting ministries they've never vetted
- Lending money to friends who never repay
- Giving to family out of fear, not freedom
- Buying things for others while going into personal debt

You must understand this: God doesn't bless giving that violates stewardship.

He doesn't honor giving that breaks order.

He doesn't reward giving done out of fear, flattery, or frustration.

He blesses cheerful and faithful givers—not frantic and pressured ones.

Stop Being Everyone's Emergency Fund

You are not an ATM for people who don't want to budget.
You are not a rescue line for people avoiding responsibility.
You are not a financial plan for those who won't create one.

Helping someone once is mercy.
Helping them twice might be grace.
Helping them a third, fourth, and fifth time while your own house suffers—that's disorder.

God may ask you to give sacrificially at times—but He will never ask you to sow into chaos while your own circle crumbles.

Ask Before You Give: Five Discernment Questions

Before you give, pause and ask:

1. Is this need in alignment with my God-given circle?
2. Does this involve someone I'm called to cover or covenant with?
3. Have I fulfilled my current responsibilities?
4. Is this gift coming from surplus—or am I robbing from another area?
5. Is the Holy Spirit leading me—or am I being manipulated?
6. Can I say yes with peace—or is this a pressured, rushed response?
7. Is this person sowing or avoiding responsibility?
8. Am I helping them grow—or helping them escape consequences?
9. Will this gift produce fruit or enable dysfunction?

10. Will it lead to long-term transformation—or short-term dependency?

Discernment doesn't make you unloving. It makes you effective.

Jesus Gave Selectively

Jesus didn't respond to every cry. He didn't meet every demand. He didn't go to every town. Why? Because He lived by assignment—not emotion.

- He healed one man at the Pool of Bethesda—while others remained sick.
- He delayed going to Lazarus even when Mary and Martha begged Him to come.
- He withdrew from crowds even when they still needed Him.

Why? Because He only did what the Father told Him to do.

If Jesus—full of compassion, love, and power—said "no," withdrew, or delayed... why do we feel guilty doing the same?

You don't need to respond to every call.
You don't need to give to every ask.
You don't need to apologize for following the Spirit instead of the pressure.

Strategic Giving Is Kingdom Giving

God wants you to be a generous person—but He also wants you to be a wise steward. He wants to give through you—but not at the expense of you.

True Kingdom giving is:

- Strategic – Planted in good soil
- Sustainable – Doesn't drain your covenant responsibilities
- Spirit-led – Guided by peace, not pressure
- Joyful – Filled with faith and fruit
- Honest – Done in integrity, not secrecy or shame

When you give this way, your generosity multiplies. You aren't drained—you're delighted. You aren't afraid—you're full of faith. Because you're giving from alignment—not chaos.

Healthy Giving = Prosperous Living

If you're constantly giving but always broke, you might not need to give more.

You might need to give better.

The answer isn't always a bigger seed—it's often a wiser placement.

Imagine a farmer scattering seed on rocks, sidewalks, and trash heaps, then wondering why nothing grows. That's how many believers give—randomly, reactively, emotionally—and then wonder why they aren't seeing fruit.

You don't need to sow into every need.

You need to sow into God's assignment for your life.

Prosperity comes when your giving is rooted in boundaries, responsibility, and wisdom.

Activation: Give From Alignment, Not Emotion

This week, pause before you give.

Ask:

- Have I fulfilled my covenants?
- Is this person in my God-given circle?
- Do I have peace—or pressure?
- Is this gift led by the Spirit—or by guilt?

Then pray:

"Holy Spirit, teach me to give from a place of wisdom, not worry. Show me where to sow and when to say no. Let my generosity be rooted in peace, purpose, and obedience. Make me a cheerful giver—not a chaotic one. I trust You to lead every act of love with clarity and power. In Jesus' name, amen."

CHAPTER 6

THE DANGER OF OPEN DOORS AND UNDEFINED LIMITS

You can't build a strong life with open doors and broken walls. In the Kingdom, boundaries protect what God is building. When you leave your circle open to anyone and everything, your life becomes unstable. Your energy is drained, your peace is stolen, and your resources are scattered. Many believers struggle—not because they're not blessed, but because they refuse to set limits.

Where there are no boundaries, there will be burnout.
Where there are no gates, there will be chaos.
Where there is no discernment, there will be defeat.

This chapter is about guarding your life—not from love, but from disorder. Because love without limits is not Christlike—it's careless. And compassion without clarity becomes a curse.

Walls in Scripture Are Not Rejection—They Are Protection

Nehemiah rebuilt the wall around Jerusalem before he

restored worship in the temple. Why? Because you can't build anything sacred without first securing it.

Walls in the Bible are a picture of order, identity, and protection.

- They marked territory.
- They kept out intruders.
- They preserved what was valuable.
- They gave leaders the ability to discern who to let in and when.

In today's world, we've mistaken boundaries for cruelty. But in God's Kingdom, boundaries are a sign of stewardship and strength. They say: "This space is sacred. Not everyone gets access."

When Hospitality Becomes Harmful

One of the most misused Christian values is "hospitality." Yes, we are called to be hospitable. But hospitality doesn't mean handing your keys to chaos. It doesn't mean letting people live in your home when they don't honor your values. It doesn't mean keeping your door open to people who don't respect your time, your energy, or your family.

Hospitality without limits becomes harmful. Examples include:

- Letting people stay at your house while rent goes unpaid.
- Giving so much food and money to guests that your kids go without.

- Hosting people who create tension, strife, or division in your home.

The home is sacred. The table is holy. If you don't guard your space, you'll lose your peace.

There's a difference between inviting people in and letting people take over. When hospitality is led by guilt instead of discernment, it produces resentment instead of joy.

Financial Boundaries: The Cost of Misplaced Mercy

One of the quickest ways to sabotage your prosperity is to give money without limits or filters. Financial boundaries are not a lack of faith—they are an expression of maturity.

Without clear boundaries, financial chaos becomes the norm. For example:

- Taking collect calls from jail multiple times a week.
- Loaning money without written agreements or follow-up.
- Covering bills for friends while your own are late.
- Buying gas and groceries for people who refuse to work.

To give without a boundary is to burn your seed.

Scripture warns against co-signing debts without discernment (Proverbs 17:18), against making rash financial commitments (Proverbs 6:1–5), and against enabling laziness (2 Thessalonians 3:10).

Mercy must always be paired with stewardship. When you

remove the requirement of growth, you replace grace with dysfunction. You give them relief in the moment—but rob them of responsibility in the long-term.

Business Boundaries: Hiring from Pity, Not Purpose

Many Christian business owners fall into the trap of compassion over competence. They hire people because they feel bad, not because the person is qualified or aligned. Then when things fall apart, they feel "mean" for letting them go.

That's not honor. That's bad leadership.

Kingdom business still requires business boundaries:

- Clear expectations
- Contracts and accountability
- Values alignment
- Willingness to correct, discipline, or release when necessary

Don't hire out of pity. Hire out of purpose.
Don't promote out of loyalty. Promote out of fruit.
Don't fund someone's dysfunction with your payroll.

When you protect your business, you protect your employees, your clients, your testimony, and your legacy.

Relational Boundaries: Everyone Can Love You—Not Everyone Gets Access

Jesus loved everyone—but He didn't give everyone the same access.

- He spoke to crowds.
- He taught the seventy.
- He walked closely with twelve.
- He revealed His heart to three.
- And even among the three, He trusted John with His mother.

Love is free. Access is earned.

If you're trying to give everyone equal time, attention, and energy—you will end up drained and distracted. That's not love. That's leakage. And it leads to compromise, comparison, and confusion.

Here are signs you've lost relational boundaries:

- People text you at all hours and expect immediate replies.
- You're afraid to say "no" because of how they might respond.
- You constantly feel anxious after conversations.
- You tolerate dishonor because you're afraid of confrontation.
- You sacrifice your covenant relationships (marriage, family) for friendships.

If access isn't guarded, your anointing will be suffocated.

Spiritual Boundaries: Protecting the Altar of Your Soul

Your time with God is not optional. It's not a luxury. It's your source. But if you don't set boundaries around your time with Him, it will get crowded out.

We often allow the urgent to replace the eternal:

- Phone notifications during prayer.
- Meetings scheduled over Sabbath.
- Responding to texts during worship.
- Saying yes to everything and then being too tired to hear God.

You can't walk in discernment when your spirit is starved.
You can't hear clearly when your schedule is loud.
You can't lead with authority when your altar is neglected.

Guard your secret place. Guard your soul.

Boundaries aren't just about keeping people out. They're about keeping your heart open to God.

When Open Doors Invite the Enemy

Not every open door is from God.
And not every open heart is healthy.

The enemy doesn't always enter through sin. Sometimes he enters through sloppy stewardship.

When you leave your life wide open:

- Bitterness slips in through unresolved conflict.
- Confusion slips in through unhealthy counsel.
- Fear slips in through overexposure to chaos.
- Lack slips in through poor financial decisions.
- Division slips in through gossip and passive leadership.

The enemy exploits open doors. It's your job to close them.

You Teach People How to Treat You

Your boundaries preach louder than your words.
If you:

- Answer texts at 2am, you're training people to disrespect your time.
- Keep lending money without accountability, you're training people to use you.
- Allow dishonor without consequence, you're training people to minimize your voice.

What you allow, you empower.

Your boundaries are not mean. They are messages. They tell people what you value, what you honor, and what you won't tolerate.

If you don't guard your circle, don't be surprised when people trample it.

Healthy Boundaries Make You More Loving, Not Less

Boundaries don't make you cold. They make you capable. They don't make you distant. They make you stable. They don't keep you from helping. They allow you to help from a place of strength.

People may not understand your boundaries—but they will eventually respect the fruit they produce.

A life in order.

A home full of peace.
A business with integrity.
A heart that can love freely without guilt or fear.

That is what happens when you define your limits and protect your circle.

Activation: Define the Doors, Set the Locks

This week, take inventory:

- What doors are open in your life that the enemy may be exploiting?
- Who has access to your time, energy, or emotions that hasn't earned it?
- Where are you leaking peace, money, or purpose through guilt?
- What boundaries need to be established, restored, or clarified?

Then pray:
"Father, teach me to set boundaries with wisdom, grace, and boldness. Show me where I've allowed chaos in the name of love. Help me to close doors that invite disorder, and to guard the gates of my life with discernment. Let every boundary I set protect what You've entrusted to me and make room for Your peace to dwell. In Jesus' name, amen."

CHAPTER 7

CHURCHES, MINISTRIES, AND THE WISDOM TO WITHHOLD

Zeal is not the same as wisdom. Passion does not equal maturity. And in ministry—whether you're leading a house church, a nonprofit, a prayer movement, or a congregation of thousands—boundaries still apply.

Some of the most financially unstable and emotionally burned-out people are not entrepreneurs or parents—they're pastors, church planters, and ministry leaders who never learned that boundaries are holy even in ministry.

This chapter is a direct call to leaders who've confused generosity with overextension, who feel guilty for investing in their local house, and who've spiritualized poor stewardship as "faith." The truth is: God is not glorified in a church that can shout in worship but can't pay its rent.

Zeal Must Be Anchored by Order

Zeal is beautiful—but it can also be reckless. In churches and ministries, zeal often looks like:

- Giving away large sums spontaneously without consulting wise counsel.
- Pouring into missions while ignoring the needs of your staff or building.
- Saying "yes" to every request for support while your own house is lacking.
- Funding events to appear "anointed" while falling behind on payroll or tithes.

These decisions aren't rooted in evil motives. They're often rooted in insecurity, pressure, or an unspoken belief that to be spiritual, you must be extravagant at all costs.

But in the Kingdom, fruit proves wisdom—not feelings.

If your giving constantly causes financial strain, if your generosity leads to confusion and chaos, it's time to step back and ask: Am I giving out of assignment or out of image?

The House Must Be Built Before the City Can Be Reached

There is a growing trend in churches to fund every cause except their own house. Leaders feel guilty building something strong and lasting. They fear being labeled as greedy or selfish. So instead of reinforcing the foundations of their own ministry, they constantly give outward—often prematurely.

This looks like:

- Supporting every local outreach initiative while staff are underpaid.
- Pouring into national or global missions while the children's ministry lacks resources.
- Giving away equipment while worship leaders are burning out.

- Renting venues for conferences while your own building falls into disrepair.

Kingdom maturity understands this: You must build the altar before you give the offering. You must reinforce your house before expanding your reach. You must secure your foundation before adding another floor.

You're not called to save the city if you're neglecting the people right in your own house.

When Giving Is Driven by Emotion, Not Assignment

Churches and ministries are often guilted into generosity. The pressure to appear relevant, compassionate, or "open-handed" can cause leaders to sow into things that look holy—but lack Kingdom alignment.

Giving out of emotion leads to:

- Disorganization
- Financial instability
- Volunteer burnout
- Confusion in mission
- Resentment among the core team

A mature church doesn't give impulsively. It gives strategically. It discerns between good soil and assigned soil. It knows that sustainable generosity requires structure.

Jesus didn't meet every need. He walked in assignment. Your church isn't called to solve every issue in the city. You're called to fulfill your assignment with clarity, integrity, and strength.

Ministry Doesn't Excuse Mismanagement

Many ministries are built on the idea that faith and finances don't mix. As if trusting God with provision means avoiding planning or structure. But faith and stewardship are not opposites—they are partners.

Ministries that ignore stewardship:

- Rarely have financial reserves
- Are unprepared for crisis
- Undervalue staff
- Undermine sustainability
- Confuse "poverty" with purity

God isn't impressed with an empty account if it was emptied through foolishness. There's a difference between sacrificial giving and irresponsible giving.

God is a God of abundance, not waste. He multiplies what we manage well, not what we give recklessly.

Leadership Must Model Healthy Boundaries

Ministry leaders set the tone. If the lead pastor or apostolic team constantly gives beyond wisdom, the house will adopt that same culture. But if leaders model discernment, structure, and financial order, the people will follow suit.

That means leaders must:

- Protect sabbath and rest rhythms
- Refuse to give under emotional pressure
- Teach biblical financial responsibility

- Practice delayed generosity until covenant obligations are fulfilled
- Invest in systems that sustain generosity long-term

You can't lead people into maturity if you're giving from immaturity.

True spiritual authority includes the authority to say "not yet," "not now," or "no."

Funding the Vision Without Violating the Boundaries

Every ministry has a God-given vision—but that vision must be built within the boundaries of assignment, covenant, and capacity.

Healthy vision casting includes:

- Clarity – What exactly are we building?
- Conviction – Why does it matter?
- Stewardship – How will we manage it wisely?
- Pacing – When is the right time?
- Alignment – Who is called to this? Who is not?

Sometimes the most anointed thing a church can do is slow down. Not every dream has to happen this year. Not every door needs to be walked through right now. Wisdom knows that timing is as important as vision.

Generosity Is Still Essential—But It Must Be Ordered

Let's be clear: This chapter is not about withholding generosity. It's about rightly ordering it.

Churches should still:

- Tithe corporately
- Give to the poor
- Support missionaries
- Partner with city initiatives
- Be a financial witness to the community

But all of that must come after the house is stable. Prosperity flows from order, not emotion. From alignment, not adrenaline.

Don't bleed out trying to prove something to people who won't be there when your team is burned out and your budget is broken.

Secure the house first. Then strengthen the city.

Stewardship Creates Longevity

You're not building a movement for a moment. You're building something multi-generational. And that requires systems, strategy, and self-control.

God doesn't just want your ministry to have momentum—He wants it to have longevity. That means saying "no" to certain requests, "wait" to certain dreams, and "not now" to certain partnerships.

It's not disobedience. It's discipline.

Honor the House, Guard the Oil

In the story of the widow and the prophet (2 Kings 4), she didn't go around giving her oil to everyone. She poured into the vessels God told her to gather. She followed a strategy that brought increase, not waste.

The oil kept flowing as long as there were boundaries—empty jars that were prepared to receive.

Churches must guard their oil.
Don't pour where there's no structure.
Don't sow where there's no alignment.
Don't sacrifice your team to maintain someone else's dream.

The house matters. The oil is holy. Protect it.

Activation: A Ministry Audit

Leaders, take time this week to reflect with your team:

1. Are we giving beyond our capacity to appear generous?
2. Are we neglecting in-house needs to meet external ones?
3. Are our financial systems built for sustainability or sentimentality?
4. Is our giving driven by the Spirit or by people-pleasing?
5. What do we need to adjust to steward our house with greater clarity and health?

Then pray:

"Father, thank You for trusting us with this house, this vision, and this team. Help us to lead with integrity, give with discernment, and

build with boundaries. Let our generosity be rooted in wisdom, not pressure. Teach us to protect what You've entrusted, to pace what You've promised, and to prosper according to Your pattern. In Jesus' name, amen."

CHAPTER 8

THE "AVAILABILITY TRAP" AND THE FEAR OF COMMITMENT

There's a growing mindset in modern culture—and even in the church—that glorifies flexibility over faithfulness. It sounds spiritual. It looks humble. But in practice, it leaves people stuck, broke, disconnected, and unfruitful.

You've likely heard it, or maybe even said it:

- "I'm just staying available for whatever God wants."
- "I don't want to commit yet—I'm open to wherever He leads."
- "I want to stay free so I can be used however He chooses."

That might sound like surrender, but in many cases, it's actually avoidance. It's fear of missing out. Fear of responsibility. Fear of losing freedom. It's a polished excuse to stay uncommitted, uninvolved, and unaccountable—while calling it "waiting on God."

But here's the truth: Real faith commits. Real trust roots. Real prosperity requires presence.

Availability Isn't the Same as Obedience

Let's break this myth once and for all: Being available to God is not the same as being obedient to God.

Availability says, "Use me however."
Obedience says, "Here I am. Send me where You said."
Availability waits passively.
Obedience moves intentionally.
Availability feels spiritual but stays neutral.
Obedience bears fruit through assignment and responsibility.

The Kingdom doesn't multiply through convenience. It multiplies through commitment.

You don't get to reap harvest in a field you were unwilling to plant in.

You don't get to walk in authority in an area you refused to commit to.

You don't get to call yourself "available" while avoiding every covenant and responsibility.

Fear of Commitment Is Often Fear of Death to Self

At the root of this "availability trap" is usually fear—fear of:

- Missing out on something better
- Being tied down
- Losing independence
- Being held accountable

- Getting hurt or disappointed

But in the Kingdom, commitment is not bondage—it's the doorway to maturity. It's the pathway to power. It's where your authority begins to grow.

God does not entrust His greatest treasures to the casually interested. He gives them to those who say, "I'm here for the long haul. I'll steward it. I'll show up when it's boring, costly, inconvenient, or slow."

Commitment is the soil where Kingdom fruit grows.

Drifting Is Not Discipleship

Discipleship requires devotion. It demands being planted. You can't make disciples while floating. You can't grow deep roots if you're constantly uprooting. Drifters don't multiply. They just observe from the sidelines while others pay the cost of building legacy.

In the early church, believers didn't "stay open" for the next opportunity. They devoted themselves to the apostles' teaching, to fellowship, to breaking bread, and to prayer (Acts 2:42). They were not spectators. They were devoted builders of the Kingdom.

Devotion is a covenant posture. It says:

- I will serve where I've been sent.
- I will love the people I've been assigned to.
- I will not run from difficulty or discomfort.
- I will grow even when it's not glamorous.

If you refuse to commit, don't be surprised when your life remains stagnant. Prosperity flows through plantedness.

The Illusion of Freedom Without Fruit

Many who avoid commitment call it "freedom," but it's really fruitlessness in disguise. They're always in transition. Always processing. Always "seeking God." But never building anything, never finishing anything, never owning anything.

Here's the hard truth:
If you're always available to everything, you're actually committed to nothing.

And when you commit to nothing, your life produces nothing.

You can't grow a business without showing up daily.
You can't raise a family without anchoring deep.
You can't build ministry without consistency.
You can't build wealth without ownership.
You can't become fruitful while floating.

Freedom is not the absence of structure. It's the ability to thrive within God's structure.

1 Timothy 5:8 — Commitment Is Kingdom Character

"If anyone does not provide for his own, especially for his household, he has denied the faith and is worse than an unbeliever." (1 Timothy 5:8)

That's a sobering verse. It doesn't just speak to family—it speaks to the heart of the Kingdom.

Providing for what you've been given—whether it's a family, a home, a calling, or a circle of influence—is the bare minimum of a faithful believer. God equates neglect of responsibility with a denial of the faith itself.

You can't say you love God and abandon what He's entrusted to you.

You can't call yourself available to heaven while ignoring your earthly assignments.

Responsibility is proof of sonship.

Calling Requires Commitment

We often talk about "calling" as if it's some mysterious, floating concept waiting to be discovered. But calling is less about hearing a mystical voice and more about showing up consistently in the place God has already spoken.

Calling requires:

- Presence
- Sacrifice
- Investment
- Repetition
- Faithfulness

The lie is that something "bigger" or "better" will come if you stay detached. But the reality is, breakthrough is almost always on the other side of full investment.

Many are one season of commitment away from explosive growth—but they won't plant, so they can't prosper.

Faithfulness Is the Bridge to Fruitfulness

God is not looking for talent. He's looking for trustworthy stewards.

The parable of the talents in Matthew 25 proves this. The faithful stewards didn't get promoted because they were the most gifted. They were promoted because they multiplied what they had.

The one who hid his talent was not condemned for doing something wrong. He was condemned for doing nothing at all.

You don't need to be brilliant to prosper. You need to be planted and responsible.

There's a Difference Between Waiting on God and Avoiding People

Yes, there are seasons of preparation and pruning. But don't use "waiting on God" as an excuse to avoid growth.

God often speaks through:

- Community
- Authority
- Spiritual family
- Covenant connections
- Assignments that require effort and follow-through

Some doors only open after you've planted roots and proven stewardship.

So ask yourself:

Am I truly waiting on God—or am I just afraid to commit?

You Were Made for Covenant, Not Constant Options

We live in a swipe-left culture. Everything is customizable, disposable, upgradeable. But the Kingdom doesn't work that way.

Covenant is not:

- Based on convenience
- Determined by feelings
- Revoked when it gets hard

Covenant says:

- I'll stay through storms
- I'll build when it's boring
- I'll give even when I don't feel like it
- I'll prosper because I chose to be planted

God blesses covenant. He promotes those who stay. He multiplies those who build through seasons of drought and difficulty. He breathes on those who say, "This is my assignment—and I will not abandon it."

Activation: Break the Fear of Commitment

This week, ask yourself honestly:

- What have I been avoiding committing to?
- Where have I stayed "available" instead of obedient?
- What's one place God has called me to plant—and I've delayed?

- What fruit have I forfeited because I feared responsibility?

Then declare:

"I break the lie that says commitment limits me.
I reject the fear of missing out.
I choose rootedness over restlessness.
I choose faithfulness over floating.
I choose Kingdom over comfort.
Lord, I will steward what You've assigned me.
I will plant, build, protect, and prosper in the place You've placed me."
In Jesus' name, amen.

CHAPTER 9

THE PROSPERITY PATHWAY

ORDER PRECEDES OVERFLOW

Prosperity is not random. It's not a divine lottery, nor is it reserved for a lucky few. In the Kingdom, prosperity follows a divine order—a sequence set by God from the beginning. It begins with alignment, flows through faithfulness, and manifests in overflow. The pathway to true prosperity is not paved with striving or sacrifice alone—it's paved with order.

Many believers are praying for breakthrough, favor, and financial increase. But they're doing it while living in relational chaos, spiritual confusion, or emotional disorder. And they don't realize: God doesn't pour into what's out of order.

The principle is simple and profound:
God fills what is aligned, not what is available.

The Divine Order of Prosperity

God's design for abundance has always been based on priority and structure. In the same way that seed, time, and harvest must follow a pattern in nature, prosperity in your life must follow a divine sequence.

Here's the Kingdom order:

1. God – Seek Him first, honor His Word, tithe, obey.
2. Self – Steward your thoughts, time, body, finances, and emotions.
3. Family – Provide for, nurture, and prioritize your household.
4. Covenant Relationships – Pour into spiritual family and trusted partners.
5. Ministry & Mission – Serve and give beyond your circle as led.

When your life reflects this divine alignment, prosperity begins to flow. But if you reverse the order—trying to bless the world while neglecting your house, or serving ministry while ignoring your health—you create cracks that prosperity leaks through.

Overflow starts at the top and flows down—never sideways, never backwards.

You Can't Build Prosperity on Disorder

The Bible says,
"Everything should be done decently and in order." (1 Corinthians 14:40)

This doesn't just apply to church services. It applies to everything in your life.

- A home without order breeds chaos.

- A business without order breeds burnout.
- A spiritual life without order breeds confusion.
- A calendar without order breeds stress.
- A mind without order breeds instability.

God is not trying to overwhelm you. He's trying to align you. Because once your life reflects His priorities, His provision can flow freely.

You don't need to beg God to bless you. You need to build the structure He can bless.

Time: The First Stewardship Test

Your calendar reveals your priorities. Before God blesses your finances, He often checks how you steward your time. Time is one of the most spiritual resources you have—and one of the easiest to waste.

Ask yourself:

- Do I give God the first part of my day?
- Do I build in rest, margin, and sabbath?
- Do I spend my time where I say my values lie?
- Do I prioritize intentional moments with my family?
- Do I guard my schedule against meaningless distractions?

Time stewardship reveals maturity. If you can't govern your day, don't expect God to hand you nations. If you won't steward 24 hours well, you won't steward $24,000 well either.

Time is the proving ground of prosperity.

Energy and Emotion: Where Is It Leaking?

Prosperity isn't just about money—it includes emotional health and energy management. Many people live exhausted, not because they're doing too much, but because they're pouring energy into unassigned spaces.

- Arguments with people who never listen.
- Worrying about things they can't control.
- Carrying emotional weight for people outside their circle.
- Avoiding confrontation and carrying silent bitterness.
- Trying to be "on" for everyone all the time.

Your emotional energy is part of your circle. If you don't set boundaries around it, it will be drained by guilt, people-pleasing, and anxiety.

Disorder in your emotional world will eventually disrupt your financial world.

Affection: Love Must Follow Order Too

The Bible says,
"Above all else, guard your heart, for everything you do flows from it." (Proverbs 4:23)

Where your affection flows, your attention and resources will follow. But many people pour their love, loyalty, and devotion into people who:

- Don't reciprocate
- Don't honor their values

- Aren't part of their God-ordained assignment

You can love everyone, but your affection—your deep emotional investment—must follow covenant, alignment, and assignment.

- Love your spouse first, not your friends.
- Invest in your children before the congregation.
- Be present for those under your roof before counseling the world.
- Let your heart be anchored in the house God has given you, not the one you're dreaming about building someday.

If your affection is out of order, your focus will be fractured. And fractured focus kills prosperity.

Build the Altar, Then Bring the Sacrifice

In the story of Elijah on Mount Carmel (1 Kings 18), before he called down fire, before he poured the water, before the offering was placed—he rebuilt the altar.

That altar was in ruins. Out of order. Broken. And until it was restored, God would not respond.

The altar represents your inner world, your alignment, your priorities.

You can't expect fire to fall when your priorities are in pieces. You can't cry out for overflow while avoiding order.

But when Elijah rebuilt the altar, placed the sacrifice in proper order, and called on God—the fire fell.

You don't have to chase fire. You have to build an altar God wants to visit.

God Fills What's in Order

Throughout Scripture, this pattern repeats:

- The ark of the covenant had to be built exactly according to God's instruction.
- The tabernacle had to be arranged according to divine design before glory descended.
- The temple had to be built in silence and order before God's presence filled it.
- The 120 had to wait in one accord before the Spirit was poured out at Pentecost.

Heaven doesn't respond to chaos. It responds to alignment.

You don't have a money problem—you may have an order problem.

You don't have a breakthrough problem—you may have a priority problem.

You don't need more hustle—you need holy habits that position you for increase.

True Prosperity Is Holistic

When God prospers you, He doesn't just increase your income. He enlarges your peace, clarity, influence, stability, and joy.

But that kind of prosperity requires you to:

- Stop ignoring dysfunction
- Start confronting disorder
- Rebuild what's been broken
- Repent of excuses
- Reinforce what matters most

This is the narrow road that leads to abundance. It's not popular. But it's powerful.

It's the path of those who've decided, "I will not beg for crumbs when I've been called to steward a feast."

Practical Steps: Align for Overflow

Here's how to walk in the order that produces prosperity:

1. Audit Your Priorities
2. List out your top five priorities. Compare them to how you spend your time, energy, and money. Where's the gap?
3. Restore What's Been Neglected
4. Rebuild the altar—spiritually, emotionally, practically. Start with your personal time with God. Then repair key relationships. Then structure your time.
5. Say No Without Guilt
6. You can't carry everything. Say no to things that don't align with your assignment—even if they're good.
7. Set Rhythms, Not Just Goals
8. Create sustainable rhythms for rest, work, family, and ministry. Prosperity flows in cycles, not just sprints.
9. Reinforce Your Boundaries

10. Guard your time, finances, and energy. Don't let people, pressure, or false guilt leak your power.

Prayer Activation: Order Before Overflow

"Father, I surrender my life to Your divine order.
Reveal the places of disorder and misalignment.
Teach me to prioritize what You prioritize.
Give me wisdom to restructure my time, energy, affection, and finances.
I break agreement with chaos, with distraction, with pressure, and with poverty.
I declare that as I walk in order, overflow will come.
As I align with Heaven, resources will flow freely.
I choose faithfulness. I choose stewardship. I choose Kingdom order.
In Jesus' name, amen."

CHAPTER 10

BOUNDARIES THAT BIRTH BLESSING

If you want to walk in lasting blessing, you must walk in lasting boundaries.

Blessing is not sustained by breakthrough moments alone—it is sustained by the systems and standards you build after the breakthrough comes. Many believers experience a measure of blessing but lose it because they never built the boundaries to protect it.

They received the promotion but didn't build boundaries around their time.

They got married but never set boundaries around their communication.

They received a financial windfall but lacked boundaries in their spending.

They were anointed for ministry but never set boundaries in their relationships.

Breakthrough without boundaries becomes burnout.

Increase without order becomes a curse.

Blessing without stewardship becomes bondage.

In this final chapter, we'll explore how boundaries aren't just protection—they are the very womb in which blessing is conceived, nurtured, and delivered.

Blessing Flows Within the Banks of Boundaries

Consider a river. A river brings life, movement, energy, and provision. But what keeps it from becoming a destructive flood? Banks. Structure. Boundaries.

The boundaries of the river allow the water to remain powerful, channeled, and fruitful.

Your life is the same. Boundaries don't limit blessing—they direct it.

They keep your emotional energy focused.

They ensure your finances flow into the right places.

They protect your home, your ministry, your health, and your peace.

Without boundaries, blessing becomes burden.

Jesus Modeled Boundary-Led Blessing

Jesus is our ultimate example of walking in overflow while maintaining boundaries.

- He loved deeply, but didn't chase after every person who rejected Him.
- He healed multitudes, but still withdrew to pray—even when people were waiting.

- He gave His life for the world, yet honored the timing of the Father in every step.

Jesus didn't run Himself ragged trying to please everyone. He stayed on mission, in alignment, and under authority.

If the Son of God lived with intentional boundaries, how much more must we?

Blessing Is Attracted to Stewardship

We often pray for blessing, but God looks for stewardship.

"Well done, good and faithful servant. You have been faithful with a few things; I will put you in charge of many things." (Matthew 25:21)

Notice the order: Faithfulness first, then increase. Boundaries first, then blessing.

Faithfulness looks like:

- Paying your bills before donating impulsively.
- Saying "no" to events so you can say "yes" to your family.
- Closing your laptop so you can rest your mind.
- Creating a budget before you sow another seed.
- Limiting your emotional availability so you can remain spiritually available.

Boundaries like these are not selfish. They are strategic containers for sustained blessing.

Healthy Boundaries Preserve What Matters Most

Boundaries allow you to say:

- "I don't have to be everywhere."
- "I don't have to carry everyone's burdens."
- "I can rest without guilt."
- "I can walk away from dishonor."
- "I can protect my family even if others don't understand."

They give you permission to preserve your priorities and walk in peace.

People may not understand your boundaries—but they will eventually see the fruit of your decisions.

Boundaries are not barriers to love. They are the frame that allows love to grow. They are not rejection. They are wise selection of what you say "yes" to long-term.

The Cost of Blessing Without Boundaries

Let's make this practical. Here's what happens when blessing shows up—but boundaries are absent:

- Without financial boundaries: Debt increases, giving becomes guilt-driven, and savings vanish.
- Without relational boundaries: Resentment builds, conflict festers, and your closest relationships suffer.
- Without time boundaries: Burnout creeps in, joy disappears, and your soul grows numb.
- Without emotional boundaries: Compassion turns into codependency, and peace gives way to panic.

In short, what was once a blessing becomes a burden too heavy to bear.

But when you establish boundaries around what God gives you, you protect the fruit and prepare for multiplication.

Boundaries Expand Capacity

One of the greatest lies is that boundaries shrink your influence. The truth is, boundaries expand your capacity.

Why? Because when your life is structured:

- You think more clearly.
- You move more intentionally.
- You give more generously.
- You lead more powerfully.
- You rest more deeply.

The less chaos you allow in, the more powerfully God can move through you.

Blessing doesn't thrive in exhaustion. It thrives in peace, presence, and purpose.

If you want God to do more through you, then let Him do more within you—starting with boundaries.

Boundaries Must Be Guarded, Not Just Given

A boundary is not just something you set once. It's something you protect continually. It requires:

- Saying "no" again after you already said it.

- Repeating yourself when someone pushes past your line.
- Walking away from relationships that refuse to honor your limits.
- Reordering your schedule when clutter starts creeping back in.
- Reestablishing a Sabbath after a busy season.

Guarding your boundaries is guarding your blessing.

Don't expect peace if you allow people, patterns, or priorities to violate what God told you to protect.

What Boundaries Produce: The Blessing Fruit

Let's end with a vision of what life looks like when you live in God-ordained boundaries:

- Peace: Your soul breathes. You're no longer overrun by pressure.
- Prosperity: Your money is working, not leaking.
- Presence: You actually enjoy God, your family, your calling.
- Power: You walk in spiritual authority because you're aligned and at rest.
- Protection: The enemy finds no open doors to exploit.

This is the fruit of boundaries that birth blessing.

Not stress. Not chaos. Not people-pleasing.
But stability, strength, and sustained overflow.

Activation: Build the Fence, Secure the Fruit

This week, ask the Holy Spirit:

- Where has blessing come, but I've failed to build a boundary to protect it?
- Where am I still operating in chaos, hoping for increase?
- What area needs a renewed commitment to boundaries—finances, time, emotions, relationships?

Then declare:

"Father, thank You for every blessing.
Teach me how to build the boundaries to sustain what You've given.
I renounce the lie that boundaries are unloving.
I receive the grace to guard what's mine, honor what's sacred, and steward what You've assigned.
Let my boundaries reflect Your wisdom and make space for greater increase.
Let the fruit of peace, joy, and prosperity multiply in my circle.
In Jesus' name, amen."

CONCLUSION

SECURE THE CIRCLE, EXPAND THE KINGDOM

You don't need to try harder. You don't need to stretch thinner. You don't need to rescue more people, say yes to more requests, or pour out what you no longer have. You need one thing:

Alignment.

Because when your life is aligned with God's order—when your circle is clearly defined and fiercely protected—everything changes.

Your peace increases.
Your focus sharpens.
Your giving becomes strategic.
Your relationships gain strength.
Your finances stabilize.
Your soul breathes again.
Your fruit multiplies.

You begin to prosper—not through performance, but

through prioritization. Not through striving, but through stewardship.

Blessing Follows Boundaries

The journey you've taken through this book isn't about pulling back from generosity, purpose, or people. It's about building the structure that sustains them.

You've seen how:

- Prosperity begins with seeking first the Kingdom.
- Authority grows where responsibility is owned.
- True love starts with honoring covenant.
- Discernment in giving produces freedom, not guilt.
- Boundaries protect your peace, presence, and purpose.
- Ministry must be built with wisdom and stewardship.
- Commitment is the bridge to fruitfulness.
- And order is the womb of overflow.

Now it's time to live it.

Your Circle Is Sacred

God has given you a circle—a territory, an assignment, a family, a business, a calling. It's not random. It's not small. It's not secondary.

It is sacred.

Your job is not to manage the whole world.
Your job is to secure the circle God gave you.

If you'll care for it, guard it, and steward it—God will increase it.

He will add to you what you need.
He will bring the right people.
He will open the right doors.
He will remove the pressure to please and replace it with the power to prosper.

Kingdom Expansion Starts With Local Stewardship

The Kingdom doesn't expand through big moments. It expands when faithful people secure what's in front of them.

Jesus didn't start with the multitudes. He started with twelve.
He didn't launch a crusade. He built a culture.
He didn't give Himself to everyone. He gave Himself fully to the ones the Father had given Him.

Secure your twelve.
Secure your house.
Secure your soul.
Secure your responsibilities.
Then—and only then—will the Kingdom expand through you with strength and longevity.

Stop Apologizing for Living in Order

You don't need to feel guilty for:

- Saying no
- Paying your bills first
- Protecting your sabbath

- Resting from ministry
- Closing your doors to dishonor
- Guarding your energy
- Prioritizing your family

That's not selfish. That's spiritual.
That's not rebellion. That's righteousness.
That's not fear. That's wisdom.

The enemy wants you exhausted and entangled. But God wants you focused and fruitful.

You Weren't Called to Save the World—Jesus Already Did

Let this truth set you free:

You're not the Savior.
You're a steward.

Jesus already did the heavy lifting. Your job is not to fix everyone or carry everything. Your job is to faithfully manage what's been assigned to you.

And when you do—when you build healthy boundaries, honor covenant, and stay aligned—God will multiply your influence, stretch your borders, and bless your obedience.

Final Charge: Build to Last

Don't build your life on emotion. Build it on truth.

Don't give from guilt. Give from alignment.

Don't stretch yourself thin. Strengthen what's yours.

Don't try to impress everyone. Please the One who called you.

Don't chase big things. Be faithful in small ones.

Secure the circle.
Build the wall.
Protect the oil.
And expand the Kingdom.

Final Prayer

"Father, I thank You for the circle You've entrusted to me.
I choose today to honor what You've given, to release what You haven't, and to walk in the wisdom of Your order.
I renounce guilt, pressure, performance, and fear.
I receive grace to build, faith to say no, and courage to stay aligned.
Let my life be a river of blessing—flowing within the boundaries You've set.
I will prosper with peace. I will give with discernment.
I will love with clarity. I will live with strength.
My circle is sacred. And I will secure it.
In Jesus' name, amen."

APPENDIX A:

DRAW YOUR CIRCLE ACTIVATION

This activation is a simple yet powerful tool to help you identify, clarify, and protect your God-given responsibilities. It's time to stop leaking energy, time, and provision into areas you were never called to carry. When you know what's inside your circle, you can guard it with boldness and give from strength—not from guilt.

Step 1: List Your Responsibilities

Start by writing down everything in your life that currently demands your attention. Include things both spiritual and practical. Don't edit or overthink—just list them all.

Consider areas like:

- Marriage or dating relationship
- Children and parenting responsibilities
- Extended family (parents, siblings, etc.)
- Your home and possessions
- Work or business obligations

- Church or ministry roles
- Financial obligations (bills, debts, giving commitments)
- Friends and social connections
- Health and personal care
- Time with God and spiritual development
- Counseling, mentoring, or helping others
- Community, school, or volunteer commitments

Once you've written them all out, move to the next step.

Step 2: Draw the Circle

Take a blank sheet of paper. Draw a large circle in the center.

Inside that circle, write down everything from your list that is truly your responsibility before God—things He has given you dominion over. These are your assignments, your covenants, your stewardship areas.

These should reflect:

- Your household
- Your children
- Your marriage or covenant relationships
- Your finances
- Your spiritual life
- Your calling or work
- Anything God has clearly told you to build, protect, or grow

Outside the circle, write down the things you listed earlier that may feel urgent or emotional, but do not belong to you in this season. These could include:

- Adults making repeated poor choices
- Friends draining your energy without growth
- Family drama you didn't create
- Ministry needs that aren't part of your assignment
- Financial requests you aren't graced to cover
- Social obligations fueled by guilt, not conviction

You can care about those things. You can pray for them. But they are not yours to carry.

Step 3: Cross Out What Is Not Yours

Take a bold marker or pen and draw a line through everything outside the circle. Not because it doesn't matter—but because it's not yours.

You're not the savior of every situation.
You're not responsible for everyone's emotions.
You're not called to fix what God didn't assign.

This act of crossing it out is prophetic. You're making a spiritual statement:

"I release what isn't mine, so I can fully steward what is."

Step 4: Pray Over Your Circle

Stand over your paper. Lay your hand on the circle.

Take a deep breath. And pray this out loud:

"Father, thank You for entrusting me with this circle.
Thank You for giving me grace, strength, and wisdom for everything inside of it.
I release every burden outside of this boundary.
I break agreement with false responsibility, guilt, and pressure.
I choose peace over striving.
I choose clarity over confusion.
I choose stewardship over sacrifice that violates order.
Teach me to guard what You've entrusted.
Teach me to say no with confidence and yes with joy.
Let every part of this circle prosper, multiply, and overflow—because it is in alignment with Your Kingdom.
In Jesus' name, amen."

This activation can be done regularly—every season, every transition, every time new opportunities arise. When you feel stretched or overwhelmed, go back to your circle.

Revisit it. Redraw it. Recommit to it.

Because secure circles birth sustainable lives. And the more faithfully you protect yours, the more powerfully God can expand it.

APPENDIX B:

PROSPERITY DECLARATIONS

Life and death are in the power of the tongue. When you speak in agreement with God's truth, you activate alignment, authority, and abundance. These prosperity declarations are designed to help you reset your mindset, reclaim your peace, and reinforce your boundaries.

Declare them boldly—daily if needed. Let your heart come into agreement with Heaven as you speak.

Declarations

1. "I am not everyone's savior—Jesus is."

I refuse to carry burdens I was never assigned to carry. I release the pressure to fix, rescue, and perform. I point people to the One who saves, and I rest in the knowledge that He is enough.

2. "My provision is in my assignment."

I do not chase money, platforms, or applause. I walk confidently in what God has called me to do, knowing that every resource I need is already prepared for the place He has sent me.

3. "I give with wisdom, not guilt."

My generosity is led by the Spirit, not by pressure. I sow into good ground, in the right season, with a cheerful and discerning heart. I am free from the fear of saying no.

4. "I build legacy through responsibility."

I steward what I've been given with excellence. I honor covenant, protect what's sacred, and lead my life with integrity. I don't just chase success—I build legacy for generations to come.

5. "God provides for what He assigns."

I trust that every assignment God gives comes with provision. I don't need to strive or manipulate. I stay in alignment, and Heaven responds. As I walk in obedience, resources are released.

How to Use These Declarations

- Morning Reset: Speak them aloud each morning to reset your mind and spirit.
- When Feeling Pressured: If someone places a demand on you that feels like a violation of your boundaries, pause and say these aloud.
- During Financial Stress: When anxiety rises about provision, repeat these to align your faith.
- Before Giving: Use them to center your motives before sowing a financial gift or offering help.

You don't need hype. You need truth spoken in faith.

These declarations are not magic—they are tools to train your soul to agree with Heaven and to silence the voices of guilt, fear, and performance.

Speak them. Believe them. Live them.

APPENDIX C:

WEEKLY BOUNDARY CHECK-IN

Sustainable prosperity isn't built in a moment—it's built through weekly rhythms of realignment. Boundaries don't just need to be set; they need to be reviewed, reinforced, and sometimes re-established. This check-in is designed to help you pause, reflect, and stay in alignment with your circle.

Set aside 10–15 minutes each week—perhaps at the end of your workweek, on your Sabbath, or every Sunday night. Use this time to quiet your heart, reflect with honesty, and course-correct with grace.

Weekly Reflection Questions

1. Where did I overextend this week?

- What did I say "yes" to that wasn't mine to carry?
- Did I do too much out of guilt, pressure, or fear of disappointing others?
- Where did I let someone else's urgency override my priorities?

2. What drained me that wasn't my responsibility?

- Who or what pulled from my time, energy, or finances that wasn't within my circle?
- Was I emotionally entangled in something God never asked me to fix?
- Did I carry burdens that belong to someone else?

3. Did I keep my covenants?

- Was I present with my spouse, children, or close relationships?
- Did I fulfill my financial, spiritual, and emotional responsibilities at home?
- Did I protect my altar—my time with God, my rest, my soul?

4. Where do I need to set a new boundary?

- Is there an area where I need to draw a clearer line?
- Are there recurring drains that require a firm "no"?
- Is the Spirit inviting me to reposition someone's access to my life?

How to Use This Check-In

- Journal your answers honestly each week.
- Pray through what God reveals, asking for strength to adjust.
- Make one concrete change—a new "no," a re-established limit, or a clarified priority.
- Invite accountability if necessary—share your reflections with a trusted spouse, mentor, or leader.

This isn't about perfection. It's about progress through alignment.

Because protected people prosper. And clarity creates capacity.

APPENDIX D:

10 SIGNS YOU'RE LIVING OUTSIDE YOUR CIRCLE

Sometimes we don't realize how far we've drifted from our God-given circle until the symptoms of misalignment show up in our lives. This appendix will help you recognize the warning signs that you're overextended, out of order, or carrying things you were never assigned to carry.

Use this list as a regular checkpoint. When more than a few of these signs are present, it's time to pause, reflect, and reestablish your boundaries.

1. Constant Fatigue

You wake up tired and go to bed even more exhausted. Even after rest, you feel drained. This isn't just physical—it's a sign that your soul is overburdened. You're doing more than God asked of you.

2. Financial Chaos

No matter how much you earn or give, you're always

behind. You feel like your money disappears without clarity or order. Often, this comes from giving beyond your boundaries or neglecting financial priorities within your circle.

3. Resentment in Relationships

You find yourself bitter, frustrated, or secretly angry at the people around you—especially those you're constantly helping. Resentment is a sign that your love has become obligation, and that you're giving more than you should.

4. Confusion in Decisions

You feel stuck, double-minded, or unsure of what God is saying. Clarity becomes foggy. This is often the result of outside voices and responsibilities clouding your inner compass.

5. Saying "Yes" but Feeling Trapped

You agree to things on the outside, but feel trapped, resentful, or powerless inside. This is a sign that you're functioning from pressure instead of conviction—and violating your own boundaries in the process.

6. Emotional Burnout

You feel numb, reactive, or emotionally unavailable—even to the people you love. Your capacity to empathize or engage feels like it's been shut off. This usually means your emotional bank account is overdrawn.

7. Guilt-Driven Generosity

You give because you feel bad—not because you feel led.

Your giving is rooted in pressure, not purpose. Over time, this leads to poverty, resentment, and confusion around generosity.

8. Poor Stewardship of Your Home

Your house—natural or spiritual—is falling apart. Maybe your marriage is suffering, your kids are acting out, or your personal space is chaotic. These are often signs that you've been investing everywhere but home.

9. Spiritual Dryness

You can't hear God clearly. Worship feels flat. The Word doesn't stir you. You're still doing all the "right things," but the flow is gone. When you're out of your circle, you're out of the flow of grace meant for your assignment.

10. Peace Only When Alone

You only feel relief when you're isolated. People feel like a burden, and rest only comes when you're disengaged from everyone and everything. This signals that your boundaries have been repeatedly violated and your system is shutting down.

What to Do If These Signs Are Showing Up

1. Return to the Circle.
2. Go back to Appendix A and redraw your circle. Clarify what's yours and what's not.
3. Repent and Realign.
4. Ask the Holy Spirit to forgive and redirect you. He doesn't shame—He shepherds.
5. Rebuild Your Boundaries.

6. Reestablish your "no." Recommit to your values. Close the doors that should've never been opened.
7. Rest and Refuel.
8. You don't recover by working harder. You recover by returning to your divine rhythm.

Living outside your circle will always cost more than it gives.

But living inside your circle will always produce fruit, peace, and prosperity.

Protect your peace.
Secure your circle.
Guard your grace.

APPENDIX E:

BOUNDARIES IN THE BIBLE

Biblical boundaries are not a modern concept—they are a Kingdom principle woven throughout Scripture. From Genesis to Revelation, God honors boundaries. He creates them, commands them, and blesses those who operate within them. This appendix gives you biblical examples to reinforce that setting limits is spiritual, wise, and necessary for sustainable prosperity.

Nehemiah: Rebuilding the Wall Before Serving the City

Before Nehemiah restored worship or reformed the people, he rebuilt the wall around Jerusalem (Nehemiah 1–6). The wall wasn't about exclusivity—it was about protection, identity, and order.

The enemy mocked and opposed the wall, just like people may mock your boundaries. But Nehemiah didn't stop. He knew that you can't bless a city if your gates are broken. He prioritized security before expansion.

Key lesson: Build boundaries first—then serve others in strength.

Jesus: Withdrawing from Crowds to Pray

Jesus regularly withdrew to lonely places to pray (Luke 5:15–16). He didn't heal everyone at once. He didn't respond to every need. He wasn't driven by demand—He was led by discernment.

Even in moments of high momentum, He prioritized solitude and connection with the Father. Jesus showed us that time with God is more urgent than the pressure to perform.

Key lesson: If Jesus needed boundaries to protect His intimacy and focus, so do you.

Paul: Focusing on Assigned Regions

In 2 Corinthians 10:13, Paul writes:

"We will not boast beyond proper limits, but will confine our boasting to the sphere of service God Himself has assigned to us."

Paul knew his territory of assignment. He refused to compete or compare. He didn't chase open doors God hadn't opened. His authority was strong—within his God-given boundaries.

Key lesson: Spiritual authority flows in your assigned space. Don't chase influence—guard your field.

Joseph: Managing Pharaoh's House Before Feeding the Nations

Joseph's rise to power wasn't immediate. He first had to manage Potiphar's house, then the prison, and only then was he placed over Pharaoh's kingdom (Genesis 39–41).

He stewarded each level with clear responsibility, wisdom, and structure. By the time famine came, Joseph had the infrastructure to distribute provision without collapse.

Key lesson: Prosperity flows to those who honor order and manage what's inside their circle before reaching beyond it.

Proverbs: Wisdom About Pledges, Laziness, and Giving

The book of Proverbs is filled with boundary wisdom:

- Don't co-sign for others' debts lightly.
- "One who has no sense shakes hands in pledge and puts up security for a neighbor." (Proverbs 17:18)
- Don't give beyond your ability.
- Proverbs warns against impulsive generosity that creates unnecessary hardship.
- Laziness leads to lack; diligence to wealth.
- "A little sleep, a little slumber… and poverty will come on you like a thief." (Proverbs 24:33–34)

Proverbs reinforces that wisdom means knowing what's yours to manage and what isn't, and setting boundaries accordingly.

Key lesson: Wisdom is practical, and it requires limits—financial, emotional, and relational.

Closing Thought

The Bible is not silent on boundaries. It is full of divine blueprints for how to live in protection, provision, and peace. Boundaries are not barriers to the blessing—they are the very structure that holds it in place.

Let Scripture shape your mindset. Let boundaries mark your obedience. And let your life reflect the clarity and prosperity of those who walk in God's appointed order.

ABOUT THE AUTHOR

Tom Cornell is the Senior Leader of SOZO Church in Washington state, founder of Walk in the Light International and SOZO Network. Tom is married to his beautiful wife Katy and lives in the Puget Sound area with her and their three kids. He has been in ministry pastoring and teaching the body of Christ since 2008.

He has a passion to see the body of Christ moving from people with an orphan mindset to that of sonship; equipping the body to do the work of Jesus resulting in seeing the Kingdom of God manifested here on earth.

www.ingramcontent.com/pod-product-compliance
Lightning Source LLC
Chambersburg PA
CBHW050530240926
51846CB00003B/763
* 9 7 8 1 9 6 9 8 8 2 3 5 7 *